WHAT WOULD HAPPEN IF...

ROBOTS BECAME SMARTER THAN HUMANS?

Written by Claudia Martin

Illustrated by Paula Bossio

WORLD BOOK

www.worldbook.com

READING TIPS

This book asks readers to ponder the question *what would happen if robots became smarter than humans?* Readers will discover how robots of the future could develop, as well as what that might mean for society and how we live our lives. Use these tips to help readers consider the ripple effects of certain actions and events.

Before Reading

Explain to readers that this book uses cause and effect to show the role computers, AI technology, and robots play in our lives. Cause and effect can help us think about why things are the way they are. It can also help us think about what might happen in the future because of our actions and choices today. Encourage readers to be on the lookout for examples of a cause and effect structure as they explore what would happen if robots became smarter than humans.

During Reading

Discuss with readers how some actions and events have multiple causes and others have multiple effects. Explain that it can be tricky to keep all the if/then scenarios straight in our minds, so it can be helpful to create a visual guide. Encourage readers to draw and add notes to their own cause and effect maps like those found on pages 24-25 and 34-35.

After Reading

After finishing the book, discuss with readers how their understandings and opinions of robots and AI technology have changed. Additionally, you can have readers respond to the comprehension questions included on page 46 and can complete the Chain of Events activity on page 47 to further extend the learning.

Visit **www.worldbook.com/resources** for additional, free educational materials.

There is a glossary of terms on pages 44–45. Terms defined in the glossary are in boldface type that **looks like this** on their first appearance on any spread (two facing pages).

Contents

Smart robots? 4
The art of smart 6
Changing work 16
Robots rule 26
The way ahead 36
Conclusion 40
Summary 42
Glossary 44
Review and reflect 46

Smart robots?

All around the world, **robots** are hard at work in factories and farms. Robots are machines with a **computer** "brain" that controls their movements. Did you know that robot "brains" are getting smarter every day? What would happen if robots became smarter than humans?

I'm getting smarter and smarter!

The computers inside robots are given sets of instructions, known as **programs.** Simple programs might tell a robot to lift a box, turn left, then put it down. The most complex programs are **artificial intelligence (AI)** programs. AI programs give instructions for difficult "thinking" tasks, like making decisions and solving problems. These programs make a robot smart!

More than 3 million robots are working in factories, making such **products** as cars.

Computers in our phones, offices, and refrigerators also use AI programs. At the moment, the smartest AI programs are not used by robots but by powerful computers, called **supercomputers.** These computers do super-smart "thinking." Could some of them be getting smarter than humans?

Robots and computers were invented to make our lives easier. Many people are excited by all the ways that they can help us. Yet other people are starting to worry that they're becoming too smart. Read on to find out more.

DID YOU KNOW?

- The first modern computer, ENIAC, was built in 1945.
- Computers contain **electric circuits**, which are turned on and off like light switches.
- The first modern robot, Unimate, was invented by George Devol in 1954.
- Powerful modern computers have over 114 billion electric circuits.
- Programs tell computers to turn their circuits on and off in different patterns, which does all their work!

THINK ABOUT IT!

If you owned a smart robot, what work would you ask it to do for you? Would you like it to do your homework? If you don't think that's a great idea, why not?

The art of smart

So just how smart are today's **robots?** In this chapter, we'll find out about the work that smart robots and **computers** are doing around the world. First, let's look at how **AI programs** make them smart.

A program is a set of instructions that tells a computer—and the robot a computer is controlling—what to do. Computers and robots can only do exactly what their programs tell them. AI programs give more complex instructions than ordinary programs, making it seem as if computers are thinking for themselves—which makes them seem smart, like a human.

AI programs instruct a computer about how to make choices and learn from the results of those choices. An AI program might instruct: If choice A gives a bad result, but choice B gives a good result, in the future choose B.

THINK ABOUT IT!

How do you make decisions? Do you think about the times when you've found yourself in a similar situation in the past? Do you think about what might happen next and how you might feel?

Let's look more closely at an AI program that plays chess. It is instructed to make each move by calculating which choice is likely to have the best result, based on all the possible moves its human opponent can make. But as the AI program plays more games, it makes smarter moves because its decisions are based on all its past wins and losses.

Ha! Beat that!

Hi! I'm Alan Turing. I was a British **computer scientist**. In 1950, I figured out a test to judge the smartness of AI programs. In the test, a person chats online with an AI program, but without knowing if they're talking with a human or a program. If the program can fool the person into thinking they're chatting with a human, the program has passed the test! In 2014, a program named Eugene Goostman passed my test for the first time.

FUN FACT!

The first simple AI programs—for playing the games checkers and chess—were created by Christopher Strachey and Dietrich Prinz in 1951.

THE ART OF SMART

AI is about more than just smart **programs:** It is also about **data**. Data is information that a **computer** can store and use. Data can be pictures, sounds, words, or numbers. Data helps to make computers and **robots** smart!

Let's consider an AI program that instructs a farming robot to tell apart weeds from useful plants. For the program to work, the computer needs to be given lots of data: hundreds of photos of weeds. Every time the robot comes across a plant, it compares information from its cameras with its photos of weeds. Then it makes the decision to kill or keep the plant!

THINK ABOUT IT

Your brain uses data something like an AI program does! When you see a cat, you know it's a cat because—in a split second—your brain checks all the data it has collected about cats.

I'm NOT a weed!

8

A common type of AI program allows someone to "unlock" their cell phone by showing their face. This is known as **facial recognition software.** This program's data is numbers: measurements of its owner's face.

The program uses the phone's **sensors,** which are devices that measure such things as light, sound, and heat. When the phone-owner holds their phone in front of their face, the program matches the sensors' measurements with the stored data—and then decides to unlock the phone!

FUN FACT!

Perseverance is a robot that is exploring the planet Mars. Its computer has stored 500,000 photos of rocks and sand, so it can recognize Martian features and decide where to go.

Mmmm ... nice and ripe!

This robot is using an AI program to choose which grapes are ready to be picked. It's comparing information from its cameras and sensors with its data about ripe grapes.

THE ART OF SMART

As we've seen, **AI** lets **robots** and **computers** do "thinking" that—until recently—only humans could do. Are some robots and computers already smarter than humans? To answer that question, we need to answer another question: What makes humans "smart"?

Unlike other animals, humans are smart enough to do math! But even basic computers can do math quicker than any human. Humans also have good memories. Yet computers already have much better memories than humans: They store and re-find **data** more effectively than we remember phone numbers, pictures, or poems.

DID YOU KNOW? The fastest **supercomputers** can do 1 quintillion (1 followed by 18 zeros) sums—such as multiplying or adding two numbers—per second.

Multiply then subtract...

If remembering and calculating are all that makes humans smart, robots have beaten us already! However, there are some human abilities that AI **programmers** have difficulty turning into instructions because they can't be broken down into simple words, numbers, or pictures.

10

Currently, robots and computers have difficulty understanding emotions. They also can't be trusted to make **moral decisions**—deciding what is kind, rather than what is simply correct. Today's AI **programs** can't show common sense, because they have no wide experience of the world. For example, if you asked a robot for "hot milk," it wouldn't know you wanted a cup of warm milk rather than a bucketful!

Supercomputers are made up of lots of connected machines, each able to perform its own work. Calculations are split between these many "brains," so they can all work at once.

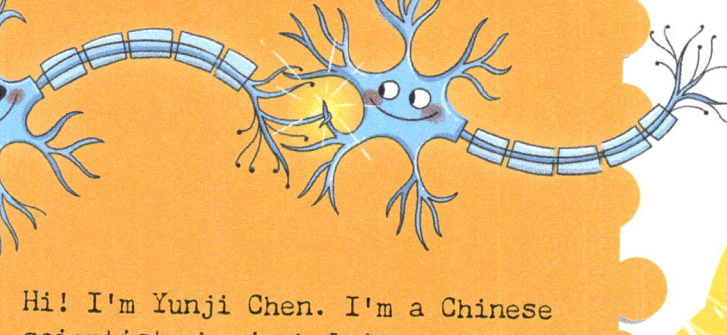

Hi! I'm Yunji Chen. I'm a Chinese scientist who is helping computers to learn new skills more quickly. At the moment, even the smartest computers and robots learn new things more slowly than humans. Human brains contain billions of tiny cells called **neurons** that easily make connections with each other. When you learn a new skill, neurons make new connections. I'm designing computers that copy this behavior, using tiny **electric circuits** instead of neurons.

THINK ABOUT IT!

What do you think being "smart" is? Is it being able to do math very quickly? Is it understanding what other people are feeling? Is it having our own unique, special ideas about the world?

A human can be a good teacher, painter, and gardener! Today's **AI programs** don't make a **robot** or **computer** good at everything, but they do instruct them to do particular tasks well. Here are some of the most common jobs that AI machines are doing right now:

No, I can't blow bubbles. Ask me a sensible question.

Search engines

When you search online—for example, for a "movie theater"—a set of AI programs known as a search engine finds websites about movie theaters. These programs decide what you're really searching for, even if you misspell. They also predict what you'll search for next, based on what you've just searched.

Personal assistants

Personal assistants are AI programs that perform tasks for their user, such as sending emails and setting timers. Assistants have microphones and speech recognition programs, so they can turn your speech into instructions, even if you don't speak very clearly. Assistants also chat by searching the web for information or choosing a funny reply they have stored.

Transportation

Self-driving cars are equipped with AI programs, **sensors**, and cameras. Programs tell them how to avoid other cars and people, as well as to remember what happened in the past, such as a bicyclist wobbling out of a bicycle lane. Fully self-driving cars and buses are not yet on sale, but some can self-drive at low speed.

THE ART OF SMART

Games

AI is widely used in computer gaming, so that a game can respond to the player's choices by changing characters, scenery, and sounds. Some games make themselves easier or harder, depending on the player's ability.

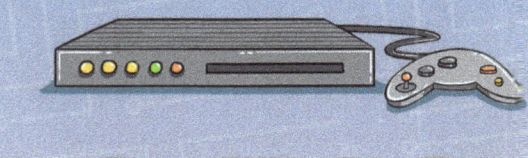

Farming and industry

Robots are used on farms to spread seeds, harvest crops, and milk cattle. In factories, robots carry materials and build products. For all these tasks, AI helps with safety by making robots react to nearby robots and people.

THINK ABOUT IT!

When they're perfected, self-driving cars may be very safe because, unlike humans, they won't break the speed limit or get distracted. Yet, in a crash, cars will have to make split-second decisions about which human lives to save. Do you think a computer program should be given that power?

THE ART OF SMART

Smart **robots** and **computers** are also starting to protect our wonderful planet and save lives. In fact, it seems as if smart machines are already making up for the ways in which humans aren't very smart at all.

Drones are equipped with **AI programs** and **sensors** that help them avoid obstacles.

My favorite animals are elephants.

FUN FACT!

An AI program called Guardian of **Endangered Species** watches the **internet** for people selling endangered animal **products**. It can identify pictures of elephant tusks and tiger claws 75 percent of the time.

Computers equipped with AI programs are watching over endangered animals. They study videos and sound recordings to identify and count elephants or whales. Smart flying robots—called drones—soar over national parks to watch for hunters.

We're smart enough to warn you when storms are approaching.

Supercomputers use **data** about wind and sunshine to predict the weather. Other AI programs monitor volcanoes and ground movements to warn of eruptions or earthquakes. If disaster does strike, drones fly over places cut off by floods or fires to spot people who need help. One of the world's smartest robots, called Atlas, was designed to rescue people from fires and accidents. It can climb ladders, open doors, turn on water hoses, and run at 5.6 miles per hour (9 km per hour).

Other AI programs are monitoring air and ocean pollution by checking data from sensors all over the planet. These smart programs are identifying where pollution is worst and figuring out which factory, mine, or construction is causing it.

THINK ABOUT IT!

If we program robots to save the planet, can we can stop making the effort to care for Earth ourselves? Or do you think we could learn something from a robot's constant, tireless work?

Why do I have to do everything around here?

Changing work

Robots have already taken over some factory and farm jobs, while **computers** running **AI programs** are carrying out some office work. In this chapter, let's look at what might happen if robots get smart enough to take over more work from humans.

AI is young! Like a child starting to walk and talk, AI is still learning. As we've seen, currently AI can't take over many jobs due to issues with learning speed, common sense, and understanding emotions. These are essential skills in most workplaces! Yet AI **programmers** are fixing these issues with smarter programming and **data.** As AI grows from a child into an adult, it will be able to do more—and there could be fewer jobs for humans.

But why would anyone employ robots rather than humans? One reason is money. Although robots are expensive to buy, they aren't paid a salary, don't get sick, and don't take vacations!

See you! I'm off to the beach!

Another reason is quality. When a robot or computer has mastered a task, it does it quickly and perfectly—even better than a human! Let's look at the example of the AI program AlphaGo, which plays the board game Go. A top human Go player, Lee Sedol, used to make money from winning competitions. When he realized that AlphaGo was so smart it beat him every time, he stopped playing. Will this problem soon face all humans with our work?

Today's robots need to be programmed and fixed by human workers, but will tomorrow's robots be able to program and manage themselves?

DID YOU KNOW?

Nine out of ten big businesses say they think AI programs and robots will help them do better than rival businesses.

THINK ABOUT IT!

If you played a game against a computer or robot that always beat you, because it was really smart, would you continue playing it or would you rather play against a human? Can you think of any reasons to take on the robot?

CHANGING WORK

Which types of jobs are smart **robots** and **computers** likely to start doing next? And which jobs could humans be doing for a while longer?

Robots have already taken over some jobs that are simple but tiring for humans. As their programming gets better, they are likely to take over more physical work, from building homes to delivering packages. Drivers of taxis and buses may lose their jobs to self-driving vehicles.

I never get bored, honestly...

I collect garbage all day ... and all night!

Around one in five of the world's warehouses already uses robots known as "pickers and packers" to find **products** and send them on their way to customers.

Computers have taken over some jobs that require difficult math and checking lots of **data**. Smart computers may take over more office jobs, such as accounting (doing math for businesses) and editing (checking spelling and facts in books and newspapers).

Jobs that need emotional understanding and **moral decisions** will probably be done by humans for a while. Teachers, politicians, and judges can keep their jobs! Currently, **AI** is also less imaginative than human writers, artists, and songwriters. However, some AI **programs** are starting to be creative. For example, ChatGPT can write about any subject by searching the **internet** for information, then editing it. For now, ChatGPT is better at writing nonfiction (about facts) than fiction (stories).

DID YOU KNOW?

In 2022, the AI art program Midjourney won a prize at the Colorado State Fair's art competition, beating its human competitors!

THINK ABOUT IT!

This book was written, illustrated, and edited by humans. In ten years, most nonfiction books may be created by AI programs. Do you think those AI-created books might be better or worse?

Hi! My name is Cynthia Breazeal. I'm a **computer scientist** who studies how humans respond to robots that look like humans, known as **humanoid** robots. I program these robots to recognize emotions by giving them data about how we show feelings through face expressions and body movements. The humanoid robots I'm designing could teach children, support people who live alone, or comfort hospital patients.

Let's imagine that we're living 30, 50, or 100 years in the future! **Robots** and **computers** are now so smart that they're doing all the work. There are no jobs for humans at all! What are the benefits to a world where humans don't have to work?

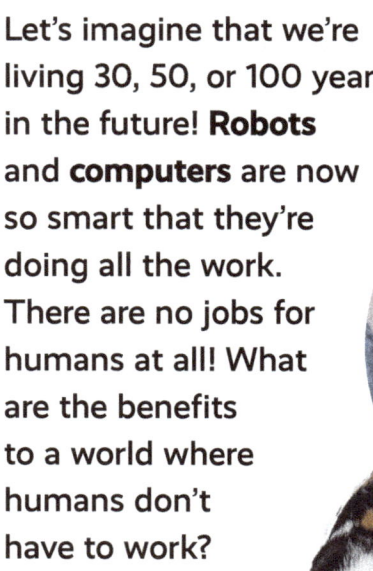

I must invent a robot to do this for me.

Super-smart future robots and computers will probably do work better than humans can! In fact, they may make the world safer and happier for humans. Robots can do all the dangerous work, such as firefighting and mining. Robots can also do the unpleasant or boring work, such as collecting garbage and cleaning.

FUN FACT!

VirtuSense is a wearable AI system that reduces by 80 percent the risk of an elderly person falling, by spotting changes in their balance and movement that could lead to a fall.

Smart medical machines will save lives. Even today, **AI programs,** such as Qure AI, have more success than humans at spotting disease in such images as X rays. In the future, robot **surgeons** will operate on patients more accurately than an unsteady human hand.

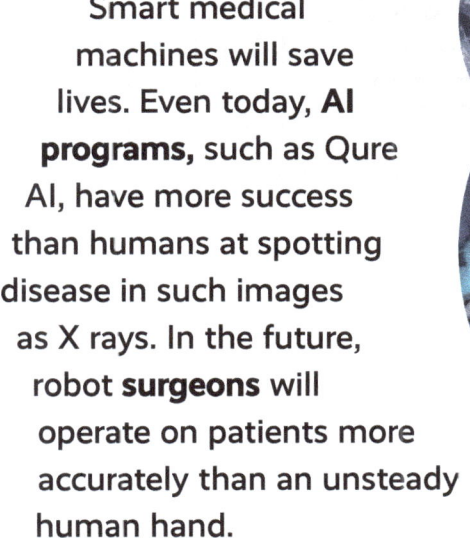

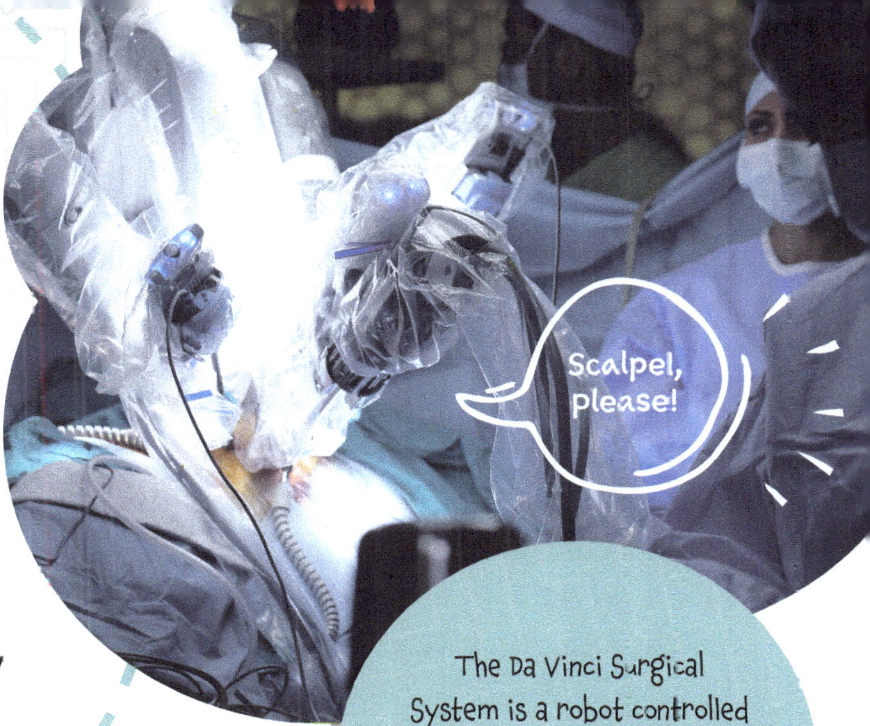

Scalpel, please!

The Da Vinci Surgical System is a robot controlled by a human surgeon as it operates on patients. One day, smart robots will operate without human help.

If humans don't need to work, we will have more time to spend with our families and friends. Every day will be a weekend! We can enjoy our hobbies all day, whether that's playing soccer or reading books. We'll always be able to find time to visit grandparents or organize a party. In fact, if we have more time for kindness, humans could grow closer to each other.

Today, children, I'm going to teach you about taking long walks ...

THINK ABOUT IT!

If you knew you would never need to get a job, would it change your feelings about school? Do you think it would still be important to go to school?

CHANGING WORK

Humans have always needed to work. To feed ourselves and our families, we've had to hunt, farm, build, or tap away at our **computer** keyboards! Not having work would be a huge change for everyone in the world. This upheaval might have negative effects …

If we had endless spare time, it might be harder to spend it enjoyably. For example, it's fun to watch TV for half an hour, but much less fun to watch it all day … every day! Many people get a sense of achievement from their work, whether they're a nurse who makes a patient smile or a businessperson who makes a sale. Without work, we would need different aims so we had a sense of purpose. If not, some people might feel bored, frustrated, or angry.

If there were no jobs for humans, how would we get money to pay for food, clothes, shelter, and fun? If smart **robots** were shared by everybody in the world, we could just ask any robot for whatever we needed without having to pay for it. However, at the moment, **AI technology** is owned only by a few thousand businesses, many of them in the United States, China, and Europe. If this remains the case, the world might become divided between people who have smart robots to give them what they need—and people who have no robots, no jobs, and no money. This would be a disaster for everyone.

Today, not everyone is sharing the benefits of smart robots. Most people can't afford a robotic vacuum cleaner, which uses **sensors** to avoid furniture and people.

Out of the way!

DID YOU KNOW?

Business researchers at the McKinsey Global Institute estimate that 50 percent of work done around the world today could already be carried out by existing robot designs and AI **programs**.

THINK ABOUT IT!

What would you do with all your spare time if you never had to work? Would you paint a picture or play the guitar even if a robot could do it better?

What would happen if robots got smart enough to do every human job?

Robots will soon be smart enough to do most **manual work**. Across the world, millions of factory, farm, transportation, and construction workers could lose their jobs. Many will retrain to do jobs that **AI** can't yet do, in offices, stores, schools, and hospitals. In fact, AI **programs** may give everyone a wider choice of jobs, for example by helping a person who can't draw to design buildings!

As AI becomes smarter, office, medical, and creative jobs could be lost. Robots become teachers, lawyers, doctors, and movie directors! However, different jobs could be created for humans by the growth of AI, including millions of new jobs in programming AI. Just like our great-grandparents could not have imagined the work humans do now with **computers**, we can't yet imagine all the jobs created by AI.

And ACTION!

If we do nothing to protect human jobs or limit the abilities of AI, eventually robots and computers could become so incredibly smart that they program, build, and test themselves. This would take away the last jobs available for humans.

THINK ABOUT IT!

Would you like to never need to get a job? Apart from earning money, can you think of anything you would gain from having a job?

Helped by robots, humans could create a fair, work-free world. Although there would be no jobs, every human would be paid an equal salary. To gain a sense of purpose, people could earn extra money or tokens by organizing community events or competing in sports. People could live longer, happier lives because robots take care of them.

If nothing were done to create a fairer world, people could be divided between those who are served by smart robots and those without robots and money. Many people could go hungry, leading to unrest and even war.

25

Robots rule

Imagine a world where **robots** are so much smarter than humans that we can't even understand how they work! In this chapter, we'll take a look at what might happen if robot abilities left human abilities far behind. First, let's find out how this could happen.

Computer scientists talk about the possibility of a "**singularity**": an explosion of robot and **computer** intelligence. The term "singularity" comes from math. It describes a moment when something grows so fast that it speeds unstoppably from 1 to 10 to 100 trillion!

You're so much smarter than mom and pop!

But how could there be a singularity with robots and computers? Here's how! Robots become so smart that they **program** new robots even smarter than themselves. These robots program smarter robots, again and again, until they are smarter than human brains can even imagine.

"I think this is where it programmed itself to fly..."

FUN FACT!

Today's **supercomputers** are 2 quadrillion (2 followed by 15 zeros) times faster than the first computers, built in the 1940's.

This possibility seems unbelievable, but humans have already programmed computers that do math and check data much faster than we can. In recent years, AI programs such as AlphaCode have even begun to write programs. Could we be moving—slowly, for now—toward the singularity?

THINK ABOUT IT!

Today's human AI **programmers** are paid to program better and better AI, so they continue doing it. If you were an AI programmer, what would you do?

"I can take over from here."

ROBOTS RULE

Let's continue imagining a world in which **robots** and **computers** have become much smarter than humans. Over the next few pages, we'll think about different **scenarios**—or possible events—this could lead to. Our first scenario is that robots have taken over our jobs, but then disaster strikes …

Robots and computers are powered by electricity. Any disaster that damaged electricity systems could damage robots and computers—and also switch off the **internet,** which is the network of wires and **wireless** radio connections that machines use to communicate with each other.

Some of the sun's energy can be seen as light and felt as heat, but it also releases other types of energy, including radio waves and X rays.

Such a disaster might be a coronal mass ejection (CME)—a sudden burst of energy from the sun. There are up to three CME's every day, usually without causing problems on Earth. However, an extremely powerful CME could frazzle Earth's electricity systems. There has not been such a huge CME since 1859. Back then, the CME did limited damage, because we had not yet invented computers and robots!

If an immense CME damaged robots, it might take hours, days, or even years to get them working perfectly again. However, if robots had taken over all jobs, humans might not have the skills needed to fix them. Even worse, humans might have lost the basic skills needed to survive, such as growing food, finding clean water, and building homes.

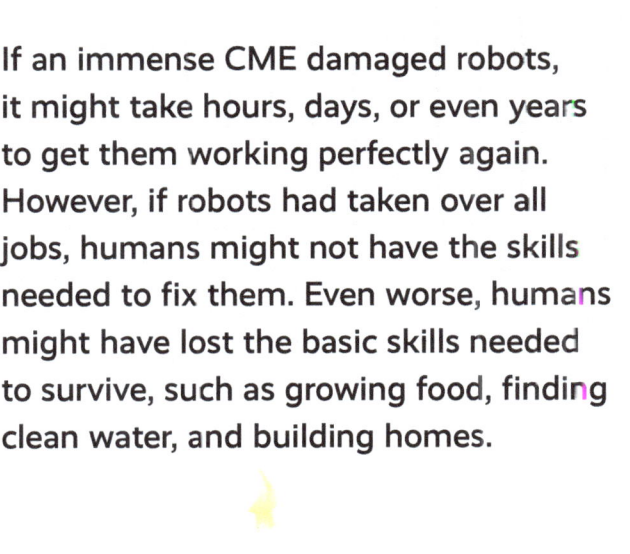

DID YOU KNOW?

In September 1859, a huge coronal mass ejection damaged telegraph systems around the world.

THINK ABOUT IT!

Humans are already losing skills because we're used to computers helping us. Relying on navigation **programs** means that many young people can't read a map. Could you use a paper map and compass to find your way to the next town?

ROBOTS RULE

Our second **scenario** is that **robots** become so much smarter than humans that they rule over us! Would our robot rulers be kind to us?

In 1942, before the first robot was even invented, the American author Isaac Asimov wrote a law for robots in a science fiction story: "A robot may not injure a human being." Many scientists think that robots should be programmed with this law. If so, robots might always protect us, however smart they become. After all, kind humans love and care for their pets!

However, today's robots are not always programmed to protect humans. This is largely because our current robots are not aware enough to understand how. A robot vacuum cleaner isn't smart enough to know what "injure" means! As robots become smarter, we can add this law into their programming, but will it help?

THINK ABOUT IT!

If you were a robot that had been programmed to protect the oceans from pollution, what would your decision-making **programs** tell you to do about humans?

30

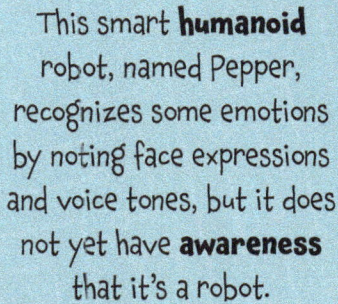

This smart **humanoid** robot, named Pepper, recognizes some emotions by noting face expressions and voice tones, but it does not yet have **awareness** that it's a robot.

A big question is: As robots become smarter, might they develop awareness? Awareness is what makes humans different from other animals. It's an understanding of the world and who we are in it. Aware robots might dislike humans because of the harm we do to the planet.

Even if we had programmed robots not to hurt us, they could delete this law! The biggest danger for humans might not be robots armed with weapons. It might be the **AI** programs that controlled everything from refrigerators to cars.

Hi! My name is Sam Altman. I'm an American **computer scientist** who has developed AI programs that write and paint. I also run the OpenAI organization, which is researching ways to develop AI that is helpful rather than harmful to humans. I think the growth of AI is unstoppable, so we must make sure it's friendly!

ROBOTS RULE

Let's look at a third **scenario!** In this scenario, we don't develop super-smart **robots** and **computers** that work separately from us. Instead, we make them part of our own bodies. We turn ourselves into robot-humans!

Animals that are the children of two different **species**—such as lions and tigers—are known as **hybrids.** By making ourselves robot-human hybrids, we could be as strong as the most powerful robot. We could be as all-knowing as the smartest **AI program.** We could design and build a house in an hour! We could know every story that was ever written!

This scenario sounds unbelievable, but a century ago, the **internet** would have sounded unbelievable. Today, American scientists are working on the possibility of "neural lace," a net-like structure that could be injected into the brain. By responding to **neurons** in the brain, the lace would let humans search the internet just by thinking.

Today, robotic prosthetic limbs can sense the activity of their user's muscles—then respond by making exactly the right movements.

Other scientists are researching **nanobots,** which are robots so tiny they can be injected into the body. These would allow us to do such tasks as storing our memories in a distant computer—or watching someone else's stored memory. Although such nanobots do not yet exist, medical nanobots are already being tested. It is hoped that, in a few years, they could heal the body from the inside—for example, by delivering drugs to exactly where they are needed.

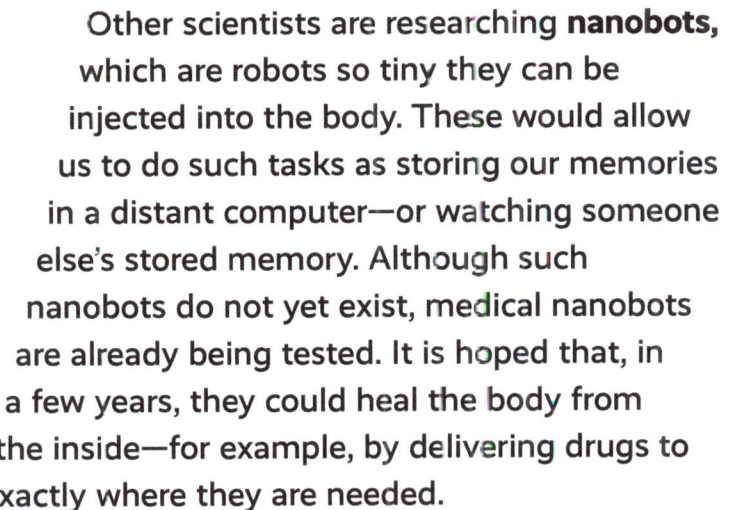

FUN FACT!

Today, the smallest working medical nanobots are 0.000005 in (0.00012 mm) long, but they have not yet been successfully injected into a human.

THINK ABOUT IT!

Our phones, which are carried in our pockets, are already extensions of ourselves, allowing us almost immediate knowledge and communication. Does becoming a hybrid take this just one step further?

What would happen if robots got super-smart?

The **singularity**—an explosion in **robot** and **computer** intelligence—takes place. Robots not only become much smarter than humans, but also become fully aware of the world, of humans, and of themselves. Robots' decisions are now beyond human control. Could their complex programming even give them something like "feelings"?

Robots rule the world, but then a disaster—such as an immense burst of energy from the sun—destroys them all. Humans no longer have the skills to fix robots or care for themselves. This catastrophe sets back human development by many hundreds—or even thousands—of years. Humans must learn how to hunt, farm, and build all over again. As we start over, do you think we should do anything differently?

Robots develop a dislike for humans, either because of our destructive behavior or simply because we look and act differently from them. Robots and **AI programs** decide to destroy humans, resulting in robot–human conflict. Which side do you think would win?

Run!

Humans see the danger of allowing AI to develop independently, so we implant AI inside ourselves. We become robot-human **hybrids,** with infinite smartness and possibilities. In fact, we are a whole new **species,** meaning that the human species dies out. However, do you think that every human would agree to be implanted?

THINK ABOUT IT!

We could replace ourselves with amazingly smart AI, which as far as we know cannot have feelings. If we did that, what would we have gained or lost? Which is more important: being smart or being happy?

Can you imagine any other **scenarios?** How about a scenario where robots treat humans extremely well? Movies and TV shows always suppose that smart robots will want to destroy us, but they might respect us as their creators. Some people are smarter than their parents, but they don't hurt them!

The way ahead

The future of **robots** is up to us! Humans are still in charge—and the decisions we make now can guide the development of **AI,** set limits, or even stop it. First, let's look at ways we can **program** AI so it's always helpful and never harmful.

As we've seen, AI can do good by, for example, protecting **endangered species.** The fact is that AI—and the smart robots and **computers** it creates—is only as good or bad as the people who program it. If a security robot hurt someone, it would be the fault of its **programmer,** not the robot. As we move forward, programmers—and the rest of us—need to question what each AI program is doing and how.

A well-programmed security robot patrols in Chengdu, China. Could a good robot be even fairer and gentler than a good human?

36

AI is also only as good as the **data** it is given. In 2016, an AI chat program called Tay had to be withdrawn because it said hateful things. Tay was supposed to learn from chatting with people on the **internet.** However, some people said hateful things to Tay—and it learned from them. This revealed a weakness in the program—and, most importantly, in human nature.

For the worst-case **scenario**—if good programming and data don't keep a robot from doing harm—they can be programmed with a "kill switch." This is a safety mechanism that switches off the machine, perhaps just by saying a single word.

Hi! I'm Joy Buolamwini. I'm a Ghanaian Canadian **computer scientist** who founded the Algorithmic Justice League. I'm challenging the ways that data and programming can make AI biased-- or show unfairness--toward people based on their race. For example, I alerted the world that some facial recognition systems found it hard to tell if darker-skinned people were male or female.

THINK ABOUT IT!

Unlike humans, robots don't have a joy of life that makes them want to stay "alive." Yet imagine a smart robot programmed to build houses, but a human threatened to stop it building by using its kill switch. What might the robot do to stop the human?

THE WAY AHEAD

Laws help to keep the world safe, fair, and functioning well. We have laws about everything from driving cars to attending school. Let's think about how creating new laws could direct the future of smart **robots**.

There are currently very few laws about robots and **AI**, but that's because—so far—there has been no need for them. However, many countries have laws about **drones** and self-driving cars to make sure they're used safely. We already have these laws because the possible harm caused by these fast-moving robots has been clear to lawmakers for a few years. If it's now becoming clear that other types of smart robots could cause harm, perhaps it's time to create new laws.

DID YOU KNOW?

Japan was one of the first countries to create a law about drones, in 2015. It required a drone user to fly their drone only where they can see it.

From the United States to China, France to Australia, many countries have laws about the standards that self-driving cars must meet before they're allowed on the roads.

38

If you were a lawmaker, what laws would you suggest? Would you ban AI **programs** entirely? If not, would you ban any AI program that could take away a human's job? Would you even ban smart robots from doing jobs that are dangerous or exhausting?

You can put out this fire yourself, if you want ...

Instead, perhaps you would consider a law requiring that any new AI program had to pass a test that showed its benefits were greater than its possible harms. Alternatively, would you focus on making laws that—rather than limiting AI—made sure that everyone, in every country, could profit equally from its benefits?

THINK ABOUT IT!

If robots become really smart, should they be considered as people? If you think so, would you be in favor of new laws that protected robots from harm and unfair treatment?

I've been working for three hours, so I'm taking my legally required break.

Conclusion

Smart **robots** and **computers** could change the world! As we've seen, they could make the world cleaner, safer, and happier for humans. However, smart robots might also take jobs, choices, and control away from humans.

What happens in the future depends not on robots but on humans and the decisions we make now. Today, robots and their **programs** are created—and their future progress decided—largely only by businesses that aim to make a profit. Our first decision is whether we let **AI** continue to be led by businesses, or whether we all need to help guide robots in the right direction.

Smart traffic light systems monitor traffic, then decide to turn traffic lights red or green! They help prevent traffic jams and accidents.

As we discovered in Chapter 1, most of us use AI programs every day, whether we notice it or not! We can all find out more about the programming and safety features of the AI we use. As we move into the future, we can choose which AI programs to use and which robots to buy.

Smart robots are a new **technology.** Today's fears about robots are perhaps like the fears people felt when airplanes were invented. At first, there were no laws about airplanes, because there was no need when they could barely make it off the runway! Then, as airplanes were perfected, we put in place laws about how they can fly safely, making them today's safest form of transportation. Airplanes have also opened up greater possibilities of exploration and learning than we ever could have dreamed. Smart robots could do just the same!

Can I help you, sir?

If you could choose, would you talk to a human or a robot sales clerk?

DID YOU KNOW?

The first airplane flight was only in 1903, but today airplanes are responsible for fewer deaths per miles traveled than cars, buses, trains, boats, or bikes!

THINK ABOUT IT!

Are you concerned about any problems that face the world? For example, are you worried about pollution or uncured diseases? Can you think of any ways that smart robots could fix these problems?

You will feel better in 0.3267 minutes.

Summary

So what might happen if **robots** got smarter than humans? Check your understanding of the possibilities described in this book.

- **Programmers** make **AI programs** that do calculations faster and faster.

- Robots and **computers** are taught to understand emotions, make **moral decisions**, and be creative.

- Lawmakers do not create laws that limit the abilities of robots and computers.

- Humans do most jobs.

- Lawmakers create laws that limit the abilities of robots and computers.

- Robots become smarter than humans.

- Helped by robots, humans live long, happy, work-free lives.

- Robots take over all work.

- Smart robots program even smarter robots, causing an explosion in robot intelligence.

- Boredom or inequality makes some humans—or all humans—unhappy.

Super-smart robot-human **hybrids** explore the Universe.

Humans advance alongside robots by becoming robot-human hybrids.

Robots destroy humans.

Together, super-smart robots and humans explore the Universe.

Robots develop a dislike for humans, because of our thoughtless behavior or because we are different.

Humans destroy robots.

Humans rebuild civilization without the help of robots and computers.

THINK ABOUT IT!

Do you think robots will get smarter than humans in your lifetime? Why or why not?

When I was young, robots were much less fun to talk to!

43

Glossary

artificial intelligence (AI)—a mix of programs and data that allows computers to perform difficult tasks, such as solving problems and making decisions. Until recently, only humans were able to do this kind of "thinking."

awareness—an understanding of the world and who you are in it

computer—a machine that can be instructed to carry out step-by-step instructions

computer scientist—a person who studies and develops computers and programs

data—information that a computer can store and use, including numbers, words, sounds, and pictures

drone—a flying robot

electric circuit—a route that electricity can flow around when the circuit is turned on. Computers have billions of electric circuits, each of which can be turned on and off. Programs instruct these circuits to turn on and off in different patterns, which completes all the computer's work.

endangered species—a group of living things that is at risk of dying out

facial recognition software—a program that identifies people by measuring their facial features, such as their nose, mouth, and eyes

humanoid—looking like a human

hybrid—a mix of two different animal species or—perhaps—a mix between a living thing and a machine, such as human and robot!

internet—a worldwide computer network, made up of countless computers connected to each other by wires or wireless links

manual work—work done by humans using strength and effort, rather than by sitting at a desk or standing in a classroom

moral decision—a choice about the right, kind, or fair action to take

nanobot—a tiny robot

neuron—a tiny working part found in the brain and in nerves. Neurons send and receive signals as tiny electric charges.

product—an object—or food or computer program—that is made so it can be sold

program—a series of instructions given to a computer, telling it exactly what to do

programmer—a person who writes computer programs

robot—a machine containing a computer that controls its movements, sounds, and other actions

scenario—an imagined series of events

sensor—a device that measures physical things such as light, sound, movement, or heat

singularity—a moment when something grows incredibly fast. An AI singularity would mean that robots and computers got very smart, very fast.

software—the programs that tell a computer's "hardware" (its physical parts, which are made in a factory) what to do

species—a group of living things that look and behave alike, such as humans or lions

supercomputer—a computer that is usually made up of lots of connected computers, each able to complete its own work, so that—together—the computers can do complex tasks very fast

surgeon—a physician who performs operations on the human body

technology—machinery, programs, and other equipment that have been designed using the scientific discoveries that humans have made

wireless—using a type of energy called radio waves to send and receive information. Wireless technology is an alternative to using wires and cables to send information.

45

Review and reflect

COMPREHENSION QUESTIONS

The art of smart
- In order to work properly, AI relies on well-written computer programs. Describe what else AL needs to help make computers and robots "smart."
- What do today's robots have trouble doing?

Changing work
- Why might people and businesses choose to employ robots instead of humans?
- Imagine people no longer had to work because robots and computers do all the jobs. How would your life change? What would you like and dislike about this new normal? can make problems for others?

Robots rule
- What do computer scientists mean when they talk about the possibility of a singularity with robots and computers?
- If the singularity takes place in your lifetime, which scenario described in the text would you most like to experience? Why?

The way ahead
- Who is Joy Buolamwini and what has she contributed to the field of AI technology?
- If you were a lawmaker, what laws would you suggest related to AI technology and robots? Why?

Conclusion and summary
- After reading this book and considering what would happen if robots became smarter than humans, what is your biggest takeaway? Why?

MAKE A CHAIN OF EVENTS!

Creating a paper chain can help you explore and visualize how cause and effect relationships can be thought of as a sequence of events.

You'll need:
- Pencil
- Scratch paper
- Pens or markers
- Stapler and staples
- Strips of paper (2 colors, if possible)

Instructions:

1. **Select a focus:** Choose a specific aspect from the book that caught your attention—it could be related to laws around AI and robots, how AI and robots are used and regulated today, or what might happen if we experience the singularity.

2. **Brainstorm causes and effects:** On a sheet of scratch paper, brainstorm and list the causes and effects related to your chosen focus. Think critically about the factors that contributed to or resulted from your focus. You can always look back in the text for ideas!

3. **Write on strips:** Write each cause and each effect on its own strip of paper. If you have different colored paper, use one color for the cause strips and the other for the effect strips.

4. **Create the paper chain:** Organize your strips into causes and effects. Start forming a paper chain to show how a cause leads to an effect. Use the stapler to connect the two strips. Continue adding cause and effect strips as links in your chain. When you've finished, you should be able to start at the beginning of your chain and read through each chain link in a logical order.

5. **Linking multiple chains:** If your focus has multiple causes or effects, you can create additional chains and link them together to show how complex cause and effect relationships can be!

Write about it!

Look at the paper chain you created and how the causes link to effects (which in turn link to other causes!). How might breaking a link in the chain impact the overall sequence of events?

World Book, Inc.
180 North LaSalle Street
Suite 900
Chicago, Illinois 60601
USA

For information about other World Book publications, visit our website at www.worldbook.com or call 1-800-WORLDBK (967-5325).

For information about sales to schools and libraries, call 1-800-975-3250 (United States), or 1-800-837-5365 (Canada).

© 2024 (print and e-book) by World Book, Inc. All rights reserved. No part of this publication may be reproduced, stored in a retrieval system, or transmitted in any form or by any means (electronic, mechanical, photocopying, recording, or otherwise) without written permission from World Book, Inc.

WORLD BOOK and the GLOBE DEVICE are registered trademarks or trademarks of World Book, Inc.

Library of Congress Cataloging-in-Publication Data for this volume has been applied for.

What Would Happen If...?
978-0-7166-5448-3 (set, hc.)

Robots Became Smarter than Humans?
ISBN: 978-0-7166-5451-3 (hc.)

Also available as:

ISBN: 978-0-7166-5457-5 (e-book)
ISBN: 978-0-7166-5463-6 (soft cover)

Staff

Editorial

Vice President
Tom Evans

Editorial Project Coordinator
Kaile Kilner

Curriculum Designer
Caroline Davidson

Proofreader
Nathalie Strassheim

Graphics and Design

Senior Visual
Communications Designer
Melanie Bender

Digital Asset Specialist
Rosalia Bledsoe

Written by Claudia Martin
Illustrated by Paula Bossio

Developed with World Book by
White-Thomson Publishing LTD
www.wtpub.co.uk

Acknowledgments

4-5	© Jenson/Shutterstock; © DeymosHR/Shutterstock	27	© REDPIXEL.PL/Shutterstock
7	© Andrey Mihaylov, Shutterstock; © gresei/Shutterstock	28	© Lia Koltyrina, Shutterstock
8-9	© Ratikova/Shutterstock; © Suwin/Shutterstock	29	© gwycech/Shutterstock; © Potapov Alexander, Shutterstock
10-11	© Kdonmuang/Shutterstock; © Unicraft/Shutterstock; © Gorodenkoff/Shutterstock	31	© VTT Studio/Shutterstock
14-15	© Leo Morgan, Shutterstock; © funkyfrogstock/Shutterstock	32-33	© Gorodenkoff/Shutterstock
16-17	© Quality Stock Arts/Shutterstock; © Lukas Gojda, Shutterstock	36-37	© Brickinfo Media/Shutterstock; © Phonlamai Photo/Shutterstock
18-19	© kuremo/Shutterstock; © Es Sarawuth, Shutterstock	38-39	© Gandolfo Cannatella, Shutterstock; © Engineer studio/Shutterstock; © aslysun/Shutterstock
20-21	© MVIDEOMEDIA/Shutterstock; © Miriam Doerr and Martin Frommherz, Shutterstock	40-41	© Zapp2Photo/Shutterstock; © Ralf Gosch, Shutterstock
22-23	© Alex Hinds, Shutterstock; © LightField Studios/Shutterstock	44-45	© Es Sarawuth, Shutterstock; © VTT Studio/Shutterstock
		46-47	© Roi and Roi/Shutterstock

www.ingramcontent.com/pod-product-compliance
Lightning Source LLC
Chambersburg PA
CBHW040848190426
43197CB00047B/2976